D1563747

**Yes, You Can Learn
Korean Language Structure
in 40 Minutes**

# Yes, You can learn KOREAN language structure in 40 minutes

by Tongku Lee

|Revised Edition|

Hollym

**Yes, You Can Learn
Korean Language Structure in 40 Minutes**

Copyright © 1998, 1999, 2004
by Tongku Lee

First published in 1998
Fourth revised edition, 2010
Fourth printing, 2014
by Hollym International Corp., USA
**Phone** 908 353 1655          **Fax** 908 353 0255
http://www.hollym.com          **e-Mail** contact@hollym.com

Published simultaneously in Korea
by Hollym Corp., Publishers, Seoul, Korea
**Phone** +82 2 734 5087          **Fax** +82 2 730 5149
http://www.hollym.co.kr          **e-Mail** info@hollym.co.kr

ISBN: 978-1-56591-300-4

*Printed in Korea*

# A CORDIAL INVITATION

**The primary goal** of this book is to provide the reader with the fundamentals necessary for the sound value of written Korean.

**The author's unique methodology** will guide you through the process, making your learning experience fun and interesting: you, too, will soon find yourself enjoying learning the basics of Korean sound structure and the letters.

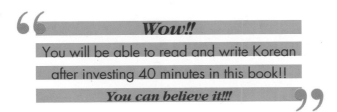

*Wow!!*

You will be able to read and write Korean after investing 40 minutes in this book!!

*You can believe it!!!*

# **A**UTHOR'S
# **I**NTRODUCTION

The methodology I have developed assumes a connection between a given culture and its writing system. I would appreciate any input or suggestions that might improve the overall quality of this learning tool. And I wish you the best of luck in your efforts to learn Korean.

I'd like to thank my wife and son who contributed to this book in earnest.

*Tongku Lee*
*Seoul, Korea*
*April, 2010*
tongkulee@naver.com

# PREFACE

- **The layout:** With a great numbers of diagrams and illustrations in  this book, general readers may easily acquire the basic idea of this book just by skimming its pages.

- **The title:** Teaching this methodology to groups of new learners of korean usually takes around 40 minutes. That is how this title came about.

- Romanization of each Korean alphabet and word is provided to help learners better understand how to read and/or pronounce the Korean letters.

# A FASCINATING APPROACH TO LEARNING KOREAN LANGUAGE STRUCTURE

By following this unique methodology, you will be able to read and write Korean in 40 minutes.

- This is a step-by-step approach. Repetition is encouraged.

- It will allow both new and experienced learners a quick and easy understanding of Korean sound and letter structure.

- Reviews at the end of each session will ensure your full comprehension.

- You will have a chance to learn from a list of useful words and expressions.

# A **U**NIQUE **A**PPROACH FOR **Q**UICK **L**EARNING

The words in Korean are made up of combinations of at least one consonant and one vowel.

**Let's suppose:** The consonants stand for men and the vowels stand for women.

1. A man and a woman get married.
2. The hypothetical family outlook:
   a. The man is responsible for protecting his family: thus, the husband always comes first in order to protect his household from any danger.
   b. However, this does not mean the husband is dominant over the wife. Rather, it is the wife who exercises influence over the husband.
   c. Thus, positioning of the consonants, either before or over, is dependent upon where the vowels are located. (i.e. if the woman stands up, the man should likewise stand up alongside; if she lies down, then he should lie over her.)

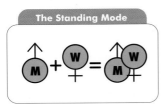

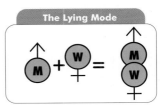

# CONTENTS

# Korean Alphabet
## (Hangeul)

# 01 Hangeul *jamo* (Korean alphabet units)

- **24 letters:** 14 consonants and 10 vowels
  cf. 26 alphabets in English

- **The 14 consonants are based on the movements of the tongue and the shapes of the mouth.**

- **The 10 vowels are divided into two modes:**
  the standing mode and the lying mode, each of which determines the position of the consonants, for example, above the vowel or below it.

Lying mode : ᅮ [nu]

＋ ＝ 누나 sister

Standing mode : 나 [nuna]

[na]

- **Each letter has its own sound value,** and the syllables are made of combinations of the consonants and the vowels.

- **Syllables are segmentations of a word.**
  \* One family = One syllable

### 14 Consonants (Men)

ㄱ ㄴ ㄷ ㄹ ㅁ ㅂ ㅅ ㅇ ㅈ ㅊ ㅋ ㅌ ㅍ ㅎ

### 10 Vowels (Women)

ㅏ ㅑ ㅓ ㅕ ㅗ ㅛ ㅜ ㅠ ㅡ ㅣ

**BASIC RULE**

❝ **a man + a woman combination** ❞

‖

a consonant + a vowel combination

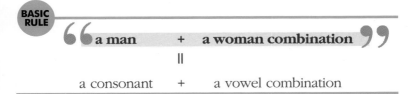

ㄱ + ㅏ → 가
[ga]

| a man | + | a woman | → | a couple |
| (a consonant) | + | (a vowel) | → | (a word) |

# How many letters does hangeul have?

1. The (      ) consonants are based on the movements of the tongue and the shapes of the mouth.

2. The (      ) vowels are divided into two modes: the standing mode and the lying mode, each of which determines the position of the consonants.

3. The combination rules are very similar to (      ) such as getting married and having children.

4. Syllables are segmentations of a word.
   * One family = (      ) syllable

KEYS : ①14  ②10  ③human life  ④one

14

# Korean-English Sound Correspondences

## 14 Consonants (Men)

| | |
|---|---|
| ㄱ | g, k* |
| ㄴ | n |
| ㄷ | d |
| ㄹ | r, l** |
| ㅁ | m |
| ㅂ | b, p*** |
| ㅅ | s |
| ㅇ | [ng]**** |
| ㅈ | j |
| ㅊ | ch |
| ㅋ | k |
| ㅌ | t |
| ㅍ | p |
| ㅎ | h |

## 10 Vowels (Women)

| | |
|---|---|
| ㅏ | a |
| ㅑ | ya |
| ㅓ | eo |
| ㅕ | yeo |
| ㅗ | o |
| ㅛ | yo |
| ㅜ | u |
| ㅠ | yu |
| ㅡ | eu |
| ㅣ | i |

\* "ㄱ" is pronounced [ g ] in the intial position, but [ k ] in the final position.
\*\* "ㄹ" is pronounced [ r ] in the intial position, but [ l ] in the final position.
\*\*\* "ㅂ" is pronounced [ b ] in the intial position, but [ p ] in the final position.
\*\*\*\* "ㅇ" has no sound value in the initial position. (e.g. 아[a] )

| 가 [ga] | ▶ | Garden |
|---------|---|--------|
| 나 [na] | ▶ | Nice |
| 다 [da] | ▶ | Dark |
| 라 [ra] | ▶ | Las Vegas |
| 마 [ma] | ▶ | March |
| 바 [ba] | ▶ | Barbara |
| 사 [sa] | ▶ | South |
| 아 [a] | ▶ | Alphabet |
| 자 [ja] | ▶ | Jamaica |
| 차 [cha] | ▶ | China |
| 카 [ka] | ▶ | Casino |
| 타 [ta] | ▶ | Time |
| 파 [pa] | ▶ | Party |
| 하 [ha] | ▶ | Harmony |

PART
02

# Consonants

## 02 Consonant Groups

Consonants were created based on **the movements of the tongue and the shapes of the mouth**.

### • The Five Subgroups

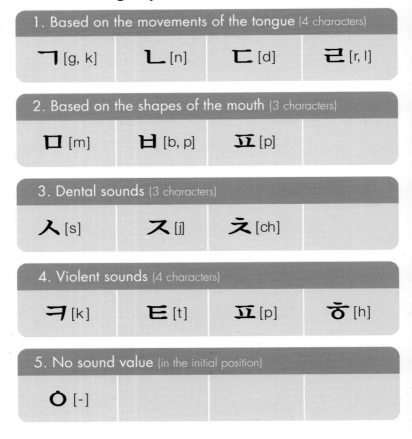

| 1. Based on the movements of the tongue (4 characters) | | | |
|---|---|---|---|
| ㄱ [g, k] | ㄴ [n] | ㄷ [d] | ㄹ [r, l] |

| 2. Based on the shapes of the mouth (3 characters) | | | |
|---|---|---|---|
| ㅁ [m] | ㅂ [b, p] | ㅍ [p] | |

| 3. Dental sounds (3 characters) | | | |
|---|---|---|---|
| ㅅ [s] | ㅈ [j] | ㅊ [ch] | |

| 4. Violent sounds (4 characters) | | | |
|---|---|---|---|
| ㅋ [k] | ㅌ [t] | ㅍ [p] | ㅎ [h] |

| 5. No sound value (in the initial position) | | | |
|---|---|---|---|
| ㅇ [-] | | | |

## Group 1 : ㄱ, ㄴ, ㄷ, ㄹ    Based on the movements of the tongue

가[ga]　　　ㄱ [기역, giyeok]

---

나[na]　　　ㄴ [니은, nieun]

---

다[da]　　　ㄷ [디귿, digeut]

---

라[ra]　　　ㄹ [리을, rieul]

---

ㄱ[g] + ㅏ[a] ⟶ 가 [ga]

ㄴ[n] + ㅏ[a] ⟶ 나 [na]

ㄷ[d] + ㅏ[a] ⟶ 다 [da]

ㄹ[r] + ㅏ[a] ⟶ 라 [ra]

∗ There is no difference in sound between "r" and "l" in Korean.

# 02 Consonant Groups

## Group 1-1 : ㄱ

가 [ga]　　　　ㄱ [기역, giyeok]

When you pronounce "가," your tongue curves from the front ceiling of your mouth and downwards to make the "ㄱ" shape.

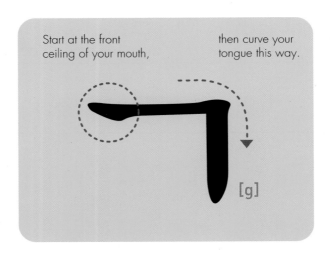

ㄱ [g] + ㅏ [a] → 가 [ga]

Shape of your tongue　+　[a] Sound

## Group 1-2 : ㄴ

나 [na]          ㄴ [니은, nieun]

When you pronounce "나," your tongue curves from the front ceiling of your mouth and downwards to make the "ㄴ" shape.

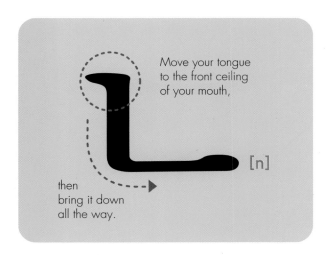

Move your tongue to the front ceiling of your mouth,

[n]

then bring it down all the way.

ㄴ [n] + ㅏ [a] → 나 [na]

Shape of your tongue + [a] Sound

Group 1-3 : ㄷ

다[da]          ㄷ [디귿, digeut]

When you pronounce "다," your tongue curves from the center of the front ceiling of your mouth and downwards to make the "ㄷ" shape.

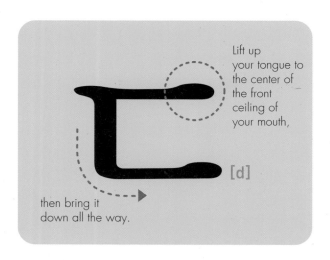

Lift up your tongue to the center of the front ceiling of your mouth,

[d]

then bring it down all the way.

ㄷ [d] + ㅏ [a] → 다 [da]

Shape of your tongue  +  [a] Sound

## Group 1-4 : ㄹ

라 [ra]          ㄹ [리을, rieul]

When you pronounce "라," your tongue slightly rolls up to make its shape somewhat like the "ㄹ" character.

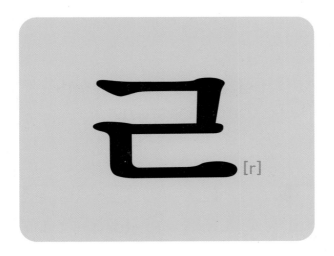

ㄹ [r]  +  ㅏ [a]  →  라 [ra]

Shape          +     [a] Sound
of your tongue

1. What are the consonants that are based on the movements of your tongue ?

ㄱ ( ) ㄷ ㄹ

2. What are the sound values of these four consonants ?

ㄱ ㄴ ㄷ ㄹ

[g] [n] [d] [ ]

Group 2 : ㅁ, ㅂ, ㅍ                    Based on the shape of your mouth

마 [ma]          ㅁ [미음, mieum]

바 [ba]          ㅂ [비읍, bieup]

파 [pa]          ㅍ [피읖, pieup]

ㅁ [m] + ㅏ [a] ⟶ 마 [ma]

ㅂ [b] + ㅏ [a] ⟶ 바 [ba]

ㅍ [p] + ㅏ [a] ⟶ 파 [pa]

### Group 2-1 : ㅁ

마 [ma]          ㅁ [미음, mieum]

The "마" sound can be produced by making your mouth into the shape of the "ㅁ" character.

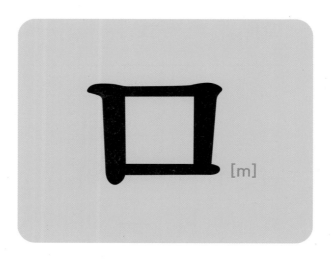

ㅁ [m]  +  ㅏ [a]  →  마 [ma]

Shape of your mouth  +  [a] Sound

## Group 2-2 : ㅂ

바[ba]        ㅂ [비읍, bieup]

The "바" sound can be produced by making your mouth into the shape of "ㅁ" character, and then moving your upper lip toward the lower lip.

(ㅁ) → ㅂ

[m]        [b]

ㅂ [b] + ㅏ [a] ⟶ 바 [ba]

Shape     +     [a] Sound
of your mouth

# 02 Consonant Groups

## Group 2-3 : ㅍ

ㅍ[pa]　　　ㅍ [ 피읖, pieup]

The "파" sound can be produced by pronouncing the "바" sound strongly.

* Please notice how "마," "바" and "파" sounds are related. Try to pay attention to the related sound while going from "마" [ma] to "바" [ba], and likewise from "바" [ba] to "파" [pa]. Then notice the phonetic connections among them.

(ㅁ)→(ㅂ)→ㅍ
[m]　　　[b]　　　[p]

ㅍ[p] ＋ ㅏ[a] → 파[pa]

Shape of your lips ＋ [a] Sound

1. What are the consonants that are based on the shapes of your mouth?

2. What are the sound values of the following consonants ?

ㅁ          ㅂ          ㅍ
[m]         [b]         [   ]

# 02 Consonant Groups

## Group 3 : ㅅ, ㅈ, ㅊ                    Dental sounds

사[sa]          ㅅ [시옷, siot]

--------------------------------------------------

자[ja]          ㅈ [지읒, jieut]

--------------------------------------------------

차[cha]         ㅊ [치읓, chieut]

---

ㅅ [s] + ㅏ [a] ⟶ 사 [sa]

ㅈ [j] + ㅏ [a] ⟶ 자 [ja]

ㅊ [ch] + ㅏ [a] ⟶ 차 [cha]

## Group 3-1 : ㅅ

사[sa]          ㅅ [ 시옷, siot]

When you pronounce "사," your upper and lower teeth come together to make the shape of the "ㅅ" character.

ㅅ [s] + ㅏ [a] ⟶ 사 [sa]

Dental sound       +       [a] Sound
like [s]

## Group 3-2 : ㅈ

자[ja]          ㅈ [지읒, jieut]

When you pronounce "자," your upper and lower teeth come together to make the shape of "ㅅ." After making the [s] sound, try to pronounce "ㅈ" by pronouncing the sound a little stronger and adding buzzing.

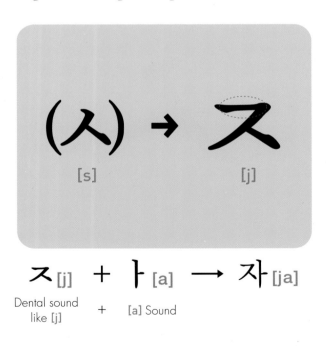

(ㅅ) → ㅈ

[s]          [j]

ㅈ[j] + ㅏ[a] → 자[ja]

Dental sound      +      [a] Sound
like [j]

Group 3-3 : ㅊ

차[cha]          ㅊ [치읓, chieut]

The "차" sound can be produced by accentuating the "자" sound.

$$(ㅅ) \rightarrow (ㅈ) \rightarrow ㅊ$$

[s]          [j]          [ch]

ㅊ[ch] + ㅏ[a] ⟶ 차[cha]

Dental sound     +     [a] Sound
like [ch]

# Review

1. What are the consonants based on the dental sounds ?

ㅅ  (      )  ㅊ

2. What are the sound values of these three consonants ?

ㅅ          ㅈ          ㅊ
[s]         [j]         [  ]

34

## Group 4 : ㅋ, ㅌ, ㅍ, ㅎ                *Violent Sounds*

가[ga]  ⟶  카[ka]          ㅋ [키읔, kieuk]

다[da]  ⟶  타[ta]          ㅌ [티읕, tieut]

바[ba]  ⟶  파[pa]          ㅍ [피읖, pieup]

아[a]  ⟶  하[ha]          ㅎ [히읗, hieut]

---

∗ "아"= ZERO + " ㅏ " combination

∗ "ZERO" : no sound value, silent

Please remember that although vowels (women) can be pronounced without a consonant (man), they cannot make up a
word without a consonant (man) ( i.e. ㅏ : ✕, 가 : ○ ).

Group 4-1 : ㅋ

가[ga] ⟶ 카[ka]          ㅋ

가[ga] + an accent point ⟶ 카[ka]

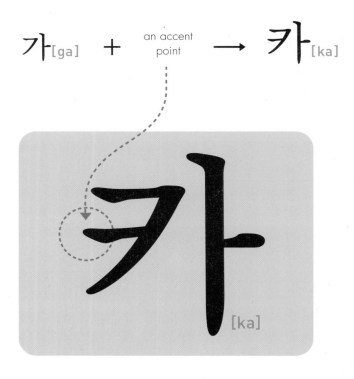

[ka]

## Group 4-2 : ㅌ

다 [da] → 타 [ta]    ㅌ

다 [da]  +  an accent point  →  타 [ta]

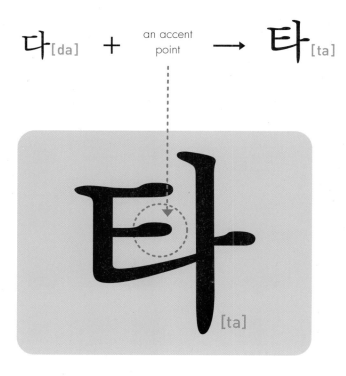

[ta]

Group 4-3 : ㅍ

---

바[ba] ⟶ 파[pa]　　ㅍ

---

바[ba]　+　an accent point　⟶　파[pa]

ㅁ　+　ㅂ　⟶　ㅍ

[m]　+　[b]　→　[p]

마　+　바　→　파

## Group 4-4 : ㅎ

$$아_{[a]} \longrightarrow 하_{[ha]} \qquad ㅎ$$

$$아_{[a]} \quad + \quad \text{an accent point} \quad \longrightarrow \quad 하_{[ha]}$$

\* " ㅏ " can be pronounced by itself, however it still needs " ㅇ " to make up the proper combination.

one consonant + one vowel = one syllable

"the simplest form of a word"

Group 5 : ㅇ

$$\text{ㅇ} \begin{bmatrix} \text{no} \\ \text{sound} \\ \text{value} \end{bmatrix} + \text{ㅏ}_{[a]} \longrightarrow \text{아}_{[a]}$$

"ㅇ" has no sound value in the initial position (father) but has in the final position (child).

- No sound value in the initial position (father) ········ 아 [a]
- Vowel (mother) sound value only ··········· 아 [a]

- Only the vowel (mother) sound value ···········
- [ng] sound in the final position (child) ··········· 앙 [ang]

- Vowel (mother) sound value only ··········· 오 [o]

- Vowel (mother) sound value only ··········· 옹 [ong]
- [ng] sound in the final position (child) ···········

1. What are the three consonants whose sounds are accentuated?

ㅋ ( ) ㅍ

2. What are the sound values of the three consonants ?

ㅋ　　ㅌ　　ㅍ
[k]　　[t]　　[ ]

3. Which consonant has no sound value?

4. Which consonant has the [ng] sound value in the final position (child) ?

# Origin of Hangeul

Hangeul is Korea's unique writing system created by King Sejong the Great in the mid-fifteenth century. It is considered to be one of the most efficient alphabets in the world and has been praised for both its scientific design and simplicity. Hangeul has been recently adopted as the writing system of the Austronesian Cia-Cia language.

In explaining the need for the new script, King Sejong said that the Korean language was different from Chinese; using Chinese characters (known as *hanja*) to write was so difficult for the common people that only privileged aristocrats (*yangban*), usually male, could read and write fluently. The majority of Koreans were effectively illiterate before the invention of hangeul.

The first Korean alphabet was proclaimed in 1446 under the title *Hunmin jeongeum* (The Correct Sounds for the Instruction of the People), after which the alphabet itself was named. The publication date of the *Hunmin Jeongeum*, October 9, later became Hangeul Day.

# Vowels

## 1. The Standing Mode (5 letters)

One arm out to the right ⟶ ㅏ

Two arms out to the right ⟶ ㅑ

One arm out to the left ⟶ ㅓ

Two arms out to the left ⟶ ㅕ

No arms ⟶ ㅣ

## 2. The Lying Mode (5 letters)

One arm up ⟶ ㅗ

Two arms up ⟶ ㅛ

One arm down ⟶ ㅜ

Two arms down ⟶ ㅠ

No arms ⟶ ㅡ

## 1. The Standing Mode (5 letters)

❶ One arm out to the right ⟶ ㅏ

❷ Two arms out to the right ⟶ ㅑ

❸ One arm out to the left ⟶ ㅓ

❹ Two arms out to the left ⟶ ㅕ

❺ No arms ⟶ ㅣ

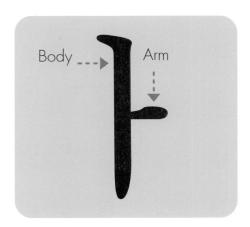

Body ---▶   Arm

\* As the vowel (woman) stands up, the consonant (man) should stands up, too. (i.e. 가)

### The Standing Mode (5 letters) – ①

One arm out to the right ⟶ ㅏ

ㄱ

ㄴ

ㄷ  + ㅏ [a]

ㄹ

ㅁ

ㅂ

⟶ 가 [ga]

⟶ 나 [na]

⟶ 다 [da]

⟶ 라 [ra]

⟶ 마 [ma]

⟶ 바 [ba]

## The Standing Mode (5 letters) – ②

Two arms out to the right ⟶ ㅑ

| | | |
|---|---|---|
| ㄱ | ⟶ | 가[gya] |
| ㄴ | ⟶ | 냐[nya] |
| ㄷ + ㅑ[ya] | ⟶ | 댜[dya] |
| ㄹ | ⟶ | 랴[rya] |
| ㅁ | ⟶ | 먀[mya] |
| ㅂ | ⟶ | 뱌[bya] |

## The Standing Mode (5 letters) — ③

One arm out to the left ⟶ ㅓ

| | | |
|---|---|---|
| ㅅ | | ⟶ 서 [seo] |
| ㅇ | | ⟶ 어 [eo] |
| ㅈ | + ㅓ [eo] | ⟶ 저 [jeo] |
| ㅊ | | ⟶ 처 [cheo] |
| ㅋ | | ⟶ 커 [keo] |
| ㅌ | | ⟶ 터 [teo] |

## The Standing Mode (5 letters) – ④

Two arms out to the left ⟶ ㅕ

| | | |
|---|---|---|
| ㅅ | ⟶ | 셔 [syeo] |
| ㅇ | ⟶ | 여 [yeo] |
| ㅈ | + ㅕ [yeo] ⟶ | 져 [jyeo] |
| ㅊ | ⟶ | 쳐 [chyeo] |
| ㅋ | ⟶ | 켜 [kyeo] |
| ㅌ | ⟶ | 텨 [tyeo] |

### The Standing Mode (5 letters) – ⑤

| No arms out | ⟶ | ㅣ |

ㅅ     ⟶     시 [si]

ㅇ     ⟶     이 [i]

ㅈ   + ㅣ [i]   ⟶     지 [ji]

ㅊ     ⟶     치 [chi]

ㅋ     ⟶     키 [ki]

ㅌ     ⟶     티 [ti]

Review

1. What are the vowels in the standing mode?

( ) ㅑ ( ) ㅕ ㅣ

2. What are the sound values of the five vowels ?

ㅏ     ㅑ     ㅓ     ㅕ     ㅣ
[ ]    [ya]    [eo]    [ ]    [i]

### 2. The Lying Mode (5 letters)

❶ One arm up ⟶ ㅗ

❷ Two arms up ⟶ ㅛ

❸ One arm down ⟶ ㅜ

❹ Two arms down ⟶ ㅠ

❺ No arms ⟶ ㅡ

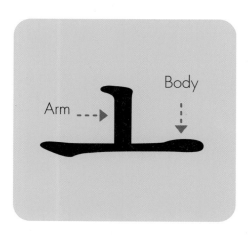

Arm

Body

* As the vowel (woman) lies down, the consonant (man) should lie over the vowel.(e.g. "고")

## The Lying Mode (5 letters) — ①

| One arm up | $\longrightarrow$ | ㅗ |

| ㄱ | | $\longrightarrow$ | 고 [go] |
| ㄴ | | $\longrightarrow$ | 노 [no] |
| ㄷ | + ㅗ [o] | $\longrightarrow$ | 도 [do] |
| ㄹ | | $\longrightarrow$ | 로 [ro] |
| ㅁ | | $\longrightarrow$ | 모 [mo] |
| ㅂ | | $\longrightarrow$ | 보 [bo] |

# 03 Vowels

## The Lying Mode (5 letters) – ②

| | |
|---|---|
| Two arms up | ⟶ ㅛ |

ㄱ ⟶ 교 [gyo]

ㄴ ⟶ 뇨 [nyo]

ㄷ + ㅛ [yo] ⟶ 됴 [dyo]

ㄹ ⟶ 료 [ryo]

ㅁ ⟶ 묘 [myo]

ㅂ ⟶ 뵤 [byo]

## The Lying Mode (5 letters) – ③

| One arm down | → | ㅜ |

| | | |
|---|---|---|
| ㄱ | → | 구 [gu] |
| ㄴ | → | 누 [nu] |
| ㄷ | + ㅜ [u] → | 두 [du] |
| ㄹ | → | 루 [ru] |
| ㅁ | → | 무 [mu] |
| ㅂ | → | 부 [bu] |

### The Lying Mode (5 letters) – ④

Two arms down  ⟶  ㅠ

ㅅ

ㅇ

ㅈ  + ㅠ[yu]

ㅊ

ㅋ

ㅍ

⟶ 슈[syu]

⟶ 유[yu]

⟶ 쥬[jyu]

⟶ 츄[chyu]

⟶ 큐[kyu]

⟶ 퓨[pyu]

# The Lying Mode (5 letters) − ⑤

| No arms | ⟶ ⚫︎ ㅡ |
| --- | --- |

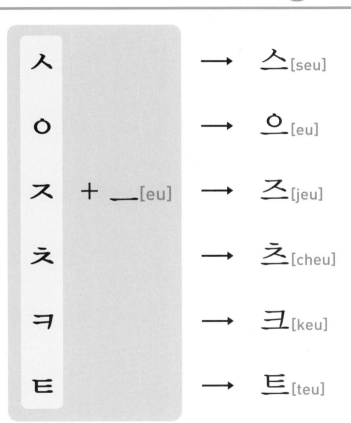

ㅅ        ⟶   스[seu]

ㅇ        ⟶   으[eu]

ㅈ   + ㅡ[eu]   ⟶   즈[jeu]

ㅊ        ⟶   츠[cheu]

ㅋ        ⟶   크[keu]

ㅌ        ⟶   트[teu]

1. What are the vowels in the lying mode ?

( ) ㅛ ( ) ㅠ —

2. What are the sound values of these five vowels ?

ㅗ     ㅛ     ㅜ     ㅠ     —
[ ]     [yo]     [u]     [ ]     [eu]

# Syllables

Consonants & Vowels

The Combination Rules

## The Combination Matrix

| | ㄱ | ㄴ | ㄷ | ㄹ | ㅁ | ㅂ | ㅅ |
|---|---|---|---|---|---|---|---|
| ㅏ | 가 [ga] | 나 [na] | 다 [da] | 라 [ra] | 마 [ma] | 바 [ba] | 사 [sa] |
| ㅑ | 갸 [gya] | 냐 [nya] | 댜 [dya] | 랴 [rya] | 먀 [mya] | 뱌 [bya] | 샤 [sya] |
| ㅓ | 거 [geo] | 너 [neo] | 더 [deo] | 러 [reo] | 머 [meo] | 버 [beo] | 서 [seo] |
| ㅕ | 겨 [gyeo] | 녀 [nyeo] | 뎌 [dyeo] | 려 [ryeo] | 며 [myeo] | 벼 [byeo] | 셔 [syeo] |
| ㅗ | 고 [go] | 노 [no] | 도 [do] | 로 [ro] | 모 [mo] | 보 [bo] | 소 [so] |
| ㅛ | 교 [gyo] | 뇨 [nyo] | 됴 [dyo] | 료 [ryo] | 묘 [myo] | 뵤 [byo] | 쇼 [syo] |
| ㅜ | 구 [gu] | 누 [nu] | 두 [du] | 루 [ru] | 무 [mu] | 부 [bu] | 수 [su] |
| ㅠ | 규 [gyu] | 뉴 [nyu] | 듀 [dyu] | 류 [ryu] | 뮤 [myu] | 뷰 [byu] | 슈 [syu] |
| ㅡ | 그 [geu] | 느 [neu] | 드 [deu] | 르 [reu] | 므 [meu] | 브 [beu] | 스 [seu] |
| ㅣ | 기 [gi] | 니 [ni] | 디 [di] | 리 [ri] | 미 [mi] | 비 [bi] | 시 [si] |

| | ㅇ | ㅈ | ㅊ | ㅋ | ㅌ | ㅍ | ㅎ |
|---|---|---|---|---|---|---|---|
| ㅏ | 아 [a] | 자 [ja] | 차 [cha] | 카 [ka] | 타 [ta] | 파 [pa] | 하 [ha] |
| ㅑ | 야 [ya] | 쟈 [jya] | 챠 [chya] | 캬 [kya] | 탸 [tya] | 퍄 [pya] | 햐 [hya] |
| ㅓ | 어 [eo] | 저 [jeo] | 처 [cheo] | 커 [keo] | 터 [teo] | 퍼 [peo] | 허 [heo] |
| ㅕ | 여 [yeo] | 져 [jyeo] | 쳐 [chyeo] | 켜 [kyeo] | 텨 [tyeo] | 펴 [pyeo] | 혀 [hyeo] |
| ㅗ | 오 [o] | 조 [jo] | 초 [cho] | 코 [ko] | 토 [to] | 포 [po] | 호 [ho] |
| ㅛ | 요 [yo] | 죠 [jyo] | 쵸 [chyo] | 쿄 [kyo] | 툐 [tyo] | 표 [pyo] | 효 [hyo] |
| ㅜ | 우 [u] | 주 [ju] | 추 [chu] | 쿠 [ku] | 투 [tu] | 푸 [pu] | 후 [hu] |
| ㅠ | 유 [ju] | 쥬 [jyu] | 츄 [chyu] | 큐 [kyu] | 튜 [tyu] | 퓨 [pyu] | 휴 [hyu] |
| ㅡ | 으 [eu] | 즈 [jeu] | 츠 [cheu] | 크 [keu] | 트 [teu] | 프 [peu] | 흐 [heu] |
| ㅣ | 이 [i] | 지 [ji] | 치 [chi] | 키 [ki] | 티 [ti] | 피 [pi] | 히 [hi] |

- Consonants (men) come before and vowels (women) come after.
- Fathers always come first.
- Fathers always come before and/or lie over everyone else.
- Occasionally, a man may have two or three wives.
- Occasionally, a man may have two or three wives and a child.
- A woman may likewise have more than one husband and/or child.
- If a woman stands up, her man should likewise stand up beside her. If she lies down, then the man should lie over her.
- The sound value " ㅇ " can be made solely by the vowel "ㅗ." However, as "a woman cannot stand up alone without her man beside her," she still needs her man (a consonant) even though he does not have any sound value.
- Occasionally, a woman may have two husbands and a child.
- Some people may favor sons.
- Some couples may have twins.

**1. A man and a woman get married and become a couple: One man and one woman make up a couple.**

Consonants (fathers) come before and vowels (mothers) come after.

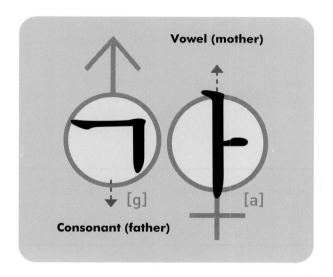

Vowel (mother)

[g]

[a]

Consonant (father)

COMBINATION

[ga]

### 2-a. The first consonant is the representative of a word.
### (The father is the representative of a family.)

Fathers always come before and/or lies over.

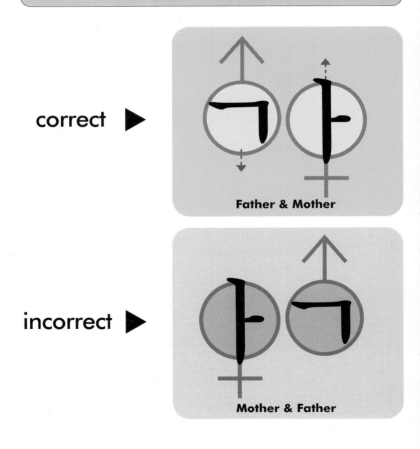

correct ▶

**Father & Mother**

incorrect ▶

**Mother & Father**

64

## 2-b. The father is the representative of a family.

Thus, the father always comes before and/or lies over everyone else.

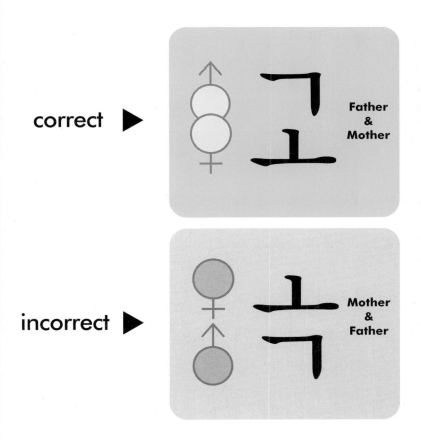

■ Occasionally, a man may have two wives and a woman may likewise have two husbands.

개, 네, 대, 베
[gae] [ne] [dae] [be]

싸, 따, 쩌, 뼈
[ssa] [tta] [jjeo] [bbyeo]

■ In all cases, the consonant (father) should come before.

■ The same two consonants may pair up.

correct ▶ ㄲ ㄸ ㅃ ㅆ ㅉ

incorrect▶ ㅄ ㄹㄴ ㅁㄴ

## 2-c. Occasionally, a man may have two or three wives.

> Man + Women (1 husband + 2 or 3 wives)

ㄱ + ㅏ + ㅣ → 개 [gae]

ㄷ + ㅗ + ㅏ + ㅣ → 돼 [dwae]

---

**Note**

When the "ㅣ" character is by itself, it can be Romanized as the letter "i."
However, when it is combined with another vowel (woman), it becomes an
"e." This rule applies to the combination rules only.(**i.e.** 이[i], 애(아+ㅣ)[ae])

## 04 The Combination Rules

**2-d. Occasionally, a man may have two or three wives and a child.**

Father + Mother(s) + Child (Man + Women + Child)

ㄱ + ㅏ + ㅣ → 개 [gae]

+ ㅇ → 갱 [gaeng]

ㄱ + ㅗ + ㅏ + ㅣ → 괘 [gwae]

+ ㄴ → 괜 [gwaen]

**Note**

ㄱ + ㅗ + ㅏ + ㅣ → 괘
[g] [o] [a] [i]  [gwae*]

* When the "ㅗ" and "ㅏ" are combined, it sounds as the [w] in English.

## 2-e. Occasionally, a woman may have two husbands.

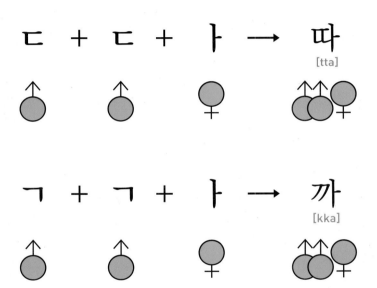

Men + Woman (2 Men + 1 Woman)

ㄷ + ㄷ + ㅏ → 따
[tta]

ㄱ + ㄱ + ㅏ → 까
[kka]

**3-a. A woman always influences a man.**

**3-b. A man's position, either before or over, depends on the woman's.**

- If she stands up, her man should stand up, too.

Man & Woman

- If she lies down, then the man should lie over her.

Man & Woman

> **Note**
>
> The standing group: 가[ga] 갸[gya] 거[geo] 겨[gyeo] 기[gi]
>
> The lying group: 고[go] 교[gyo] 구[gu] 규[gyu] 그[geu]

## 3-c. A woman may influence her man, yet she cannot stand up alone without her man alongside her.

> The sound value " ㅇ " can be made solely by the vowel "ㅗ." However, as a waman cannot stand up alone without her man alongside her, she still needs her man (a consonant), though he has no sound value.

So, we use ZERO, " ㅇ " for this.

아 ➜ ZERO + [a] ⟶ [a]

야 ➜ ZERO + [ya] ⟶ [ya]

오 ➜ ZERO + [o] ⟶ [o]

요 ➜ ZERO + [yo] ⟶ [yo]

---

**Note**

Syllables that start with " ㅇ " (ZERO) have no sound value as consonants.
They only have vowel sounds.

---

**3-d. Occasionally, a woman may have two husbands and a child.**

Fathers + Mother + Child
(2 Men + 1 Woman + 1 Child)

ㄷ + ㄷ + ㅏ → 따 [tta]

+ ㄹ → 딸 [ttal]

ㄱ + ㄱ + ㅏ → 까 [kka]

+ ㅁ → 깜 [kkam]

\* **Some couples have two children.**

   **a. Sometimes a couple has twins (dual consonants).**

   **b. Children (dual consonants) are never to come before as long as their parents are alive.**

The father (consonant) comes before,
the mother (vowel) after,
and the children (dual consonants) follow.

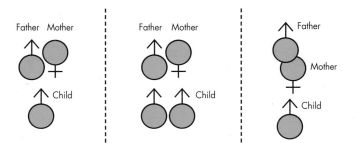

박, 선, 당   닭, 밝, 삶   손, 봉, 국

[bak] [seon] [dang]   [dak] [bak] [sam]   [son] [bong] [guk]

# 04 The Combination Rules

**4-a. Boys may be "preferred" over girls by some parents.**

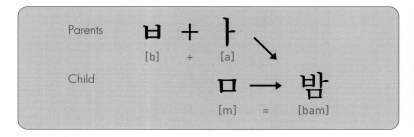

Parents    ㅂ + ㅏ
          [b]   +   [a]

Child    ㅁ → 밤
          [m]   =   [bam]

■ Father comes before, mother after. Then the child follows.

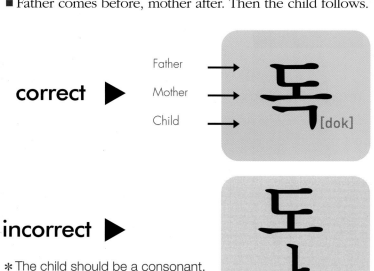

**correct** ▶

Father →
Mother →
Child →

독 [dok]

**incorrect** ▶

도ㅏ

\* The child should be a consonant, not a vowel.

## 4-b. Some families may have twins.

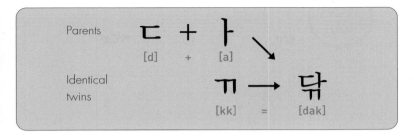

Parents  ㄷ + ㅏ
         [d] + [a]

Identical twins  ㄲ → 닦
                 [kk] = [dak]

Parents  ㄷ + ㅏ
         [d] + [a]

Two-egg twins  ㄺ → 닭
               [rk] = [dak]

＊More than two children are not necessary for the purpose of this study.

---

**Note**

In instances where there are double consonants, ( **e.g.** ㅆ) or two separate consonants ( **e.g.** ㄺ ), there are two English letters corresponding to the same number of Korean letters, according to this particular Romanization system. It should be noted, however, that only one letter is pronounced. So, as in the case of 닭, although it is written "dark" in English, it is simply pronounced [dak].

# Korean Family

In the past, most of the Korean households were an "extended family," which consists of old parents, their first son and his wife. Because infant mortality was high and a big family was thought of as a blessing, having many children was desired. However, the rapid industrialization and urbanization of the country in the 1960s and 1970s were accompanied by an effective campaign to enhance birth control, so the average number of children in a family has dramatically decreased to two or less since the 1980s.

Due to the long Confucian tradition of the eldest son taking over as head of the family, a preference for sons was prevalent in Korea. To tackle the problem of male preference, the government has completely rewritten family-related laws in a way that ensures equality for sons and daughters in terms of inheritance.

These days, young married couples prefer to separate from their extended families and live in their own homes. Now, almost all families are couple-centered nuclear ones.

# Syllables &
# Word Segments

Syllables & Word Segments

* "One Family = One Syllable" principle

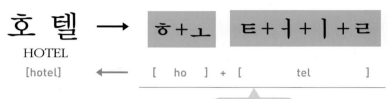

호 텔 ⟶ ㅎ+ㅗ  ㅌ+ㅓ+ㅣ+ㄹ
HOTEL
[hotel] ⟵ [ ho ] + [ tel ]

Two Syllables

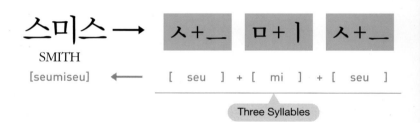

스미스 ⟶ ㅅ+ㅡ  ㅁ+ㅣ  ㅅ+ㅡ
SMITH
[seumiseu] ⟵ [ seu ] + [ mi ] + [ seu ]

Three Syllables

존 슨 ⟶ ㅈ+ㅗ+ㄴ  ㅅ+ㅡ+ㄴ
JOHNSON
[jonseun] ⟵ [ jon ] + [ seun ]

78

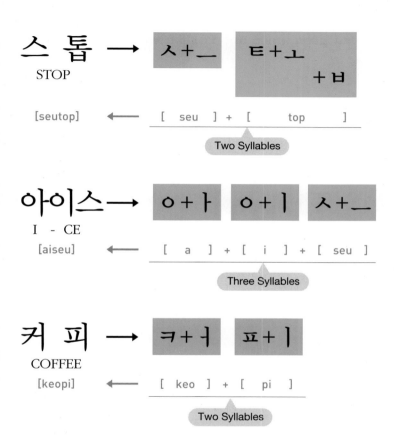

스 톱 → ㅅ+ㅡ    ㅌ+ㅗ +ㅂ
STOP

[seutop] ← [ seu ] + [ top ]

Two Syllables

아이스→ ㅇ+ㅏ  ㅇ+ㅣ  ㅅ+ㅡ
I - CE

[aiseu] ← [ a ] + [ i ] + [ seu ]

Three Syllables

커 피 → ㅋ+ㅓ  ㅍ+ㅣ
COFFEE

[keopi] ← [ keo ] + [ pi ]

Two Syllables

\* One couple (family) has one syllable.

Syllables are segments of a word. In the following case, you can pronounce one English word in two different ways.

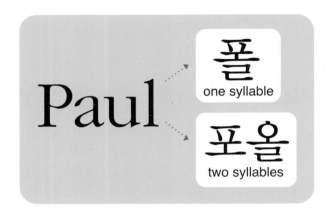

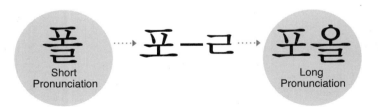

# Vocabulary:
# A Selected List

| Numbers | Native Korean Numbers | | Sino-Korean Numbers | |
|:---:|:---:|:---:|:---:|:---:|
| 1 | 하나 | [hana] | 일 | [il] |
| 2 | 둘 | [dul] | 이 | [i] |
| 3 | 셋 | [set] | 삼 | [sam] |
| 4 | 넷 | [net] | 사 | [sa] |
| 5 | 다섯 | [daseot] | 오 | [o] |
| 6 | 여섯 | [yeoseot] | 육 | [yuk] |
| 7 | 일곱 | [ilgop] | 칠 | [chil] |

| Numbers | Native Korean Numbers | | Sino-Korean Numbers | |
|---------|-----------|------------|-----------|-----------|
| 8 | 여덟 | [yeodeol] | 팔 | [pal] |
| 9 | 아홉 | [ahop] | 구 | [gu] |
| 10 | 열 | [yeol] | 십 | [sip] |
| 11 | 열하나 | [yeolhana] | 십일 | [sibil] |
| 12 | 열둘 | [yeoldul] | 십이 | [sibi] |
| 13 | 열셋 | [yeolset] | 십삼 | [sipsam] |
| 20 | 스물 | [seumul] | 이십 | [isip] |

| Numbers | Native Korean Numbers | | Sino-Korean Numbers | |
|---------|------------|------------|------------|------------|
| 21 | 스물하나 | [seumul hana] | 이십일 | [isibil] |
| 22 | 스물둘 | [seumul dul] | 이십이 | [isibi] |
| 30 | 서른 | [seoreun] | 삼십 | [samsip] |
| 40 | 마흔 | [maheun] | 사십 | [sasip] |
| 50 | 쉰 | [swin] | 오십 | [osip] |
| 60 | 예순 | [yesun] | 육십 | [yuksip] |
| 70 | 이른 | [ilheun] | 칠십 | [chilsip] |

| Numbers | Native Korean Numbers | | Sino-Korean Numbers | |
|---|---|---|---|---|
| 80 | 여든 | [yeodeun] | 팔십 | [palsip] |
| 90 | 아흔 | [aheun] | 구십 | [gusip] |
| 100 | 백 | [baek] | 백 | [baek] |
| 1,000 | 천 | [cheon] | 천 | [cheon] |
| 10,000 | 만 | [man] | 만 | [man] |
| 100,000 | 십만 | [simman] | 십만 | [simman] |
| 1,000,000 | 백만 | [baengman] | 백만 | [baengman] |

# 06 Currency Unit

**Basic unit : won** (원, ₩)

## Coins

| | | |
|---|---|---|
| ₩ 10 | 십원 [sibwon] | |
| ₩ 50 | 오십원 [osibwon] | |
| ₩ 100 | 백원 [baegwon] | |
| ₩ 500 | 오백원 [obaegwon] | |

## Bills

| | | |
|---|---|---|
| ₩ 1,000 | 천원 [cheonwon] | |
| ₩ 5,000 | 오천원 [ocheonwon] | |
| ₩ 10,000 | 만원 [manwon] | |
| ₩ 50,000 | 오만원 [omanwon] | |

| 1 | 10 | 100 | 1000 | 10,000 |
|---|---|---|---|---|
| 일 | 십 | 백 | 천 | 만 |
| [ il ] | [ sip ] | [ baek ] | [ cheon ] | [ man ] |

| 100,000 | 1,000,000 | 10,000,000 |
|---|---|---|
| 십만 | 백만 | 천만 |
| [ simman ] | [ baengman ] | [ cheonman ] |

| 100,000,000 | 1,000,000,000 |
|---|---|
| 일 억 | 십 억 |
| [ ireok ] | [ sibeok ] |

| 10,000,000,000 | 100,000,000,000 |
|---|---|
| 백 억 | 천 억 |
| [ baegeok ] | [ cheoneok ] |

| 1,000,000,000,000 |
|---|
| 일 조 |
| [ iljo ] |

| 10,000,000,000,000 |
|---|
| 십 조 |
| [ sipjo ] |

- To address someone with his or her full name, the family name comes first, then the given name.

  ▸ The three most common family names are Kim (김), Lee (이) and Park (박).
  ▸ Usually a full name has three syllables:
    • The first syllable is **the family name**. ←┄┄┄┄
    • The two syllables that follow are **the given name**. ←┄┄

    [kim] [yeoungbok]
    김 영복

  ▸ Some given names have only one syllable:
    • **The family name** comes first. ←┄┄┄
    • **The given name** follows. ←┄┄┄┄┄

    [lee] [jun]
    이 준

  ▸ A few family names have two syllables: ┄┄
    • The first two syllables are **the family name**.
    • The two syllables that follow are **the given name**. ←┄┄┄

    [hwangbo] [jieun]
    황보 지은

- Addressing someone with their family name is considered much more polite.

- Except for children and those who are younger than you, people are not to be addressed with their given names only, but rather with their full names or titles.

- Names hold a special meaning to Koreans, thus people respect others' names and expect the same from others in return.

|  | Familly Name | Given Name |
|---|---|---|
| Three Syllables | 김 [kim] | 대중 [daejung] |
| Three Syllables | 박 [bak] | 정희 [jeonghui] |
| Two Syllables | 김 [kim] | 영 [young] |
| Four Syllables | 선우 [seonu] | 정선 [jeongseon] |

| | | |
|---|---|---|
| Paul | ▶ | 폴 [ pol ] |
| Jane | ▶ | 제인 [ jein ] |
| Robert | ▶ | 로버트 [ robeateu ] |
| Diana | ▶ | 다이아나 [ daiana ] |
| Tom | ▶ | 톰 [ tom ] |
| Juliet | ▶ | 줄리엣 [ julliet ] |
| Peter | ▶ | 피터 [ piteo ] |
| Anna | ▶ | 애나 [ aena ] |
| David | ▶ | 데이빗 [ deibideu ] |
| Johan | ▶ | 요한 [ yohan ] |
| Julia | ▶ | 줄리아 [ jullia ] |
| Margaret | ▶ | 마가렛 [ magaret ] |
| Maria | ▶ | 마리아 [ maria ] |

Between the 14th-20th centuries (1392~1910)

The last dynasty of Korea.
The name means "Morning Calm."

Between the 10th-14th centuries

The name means "High and Beautiful."
During its time, Korea had made its initial introduction to Europe, and since then the name "Corea/Korea" has become known to the world.

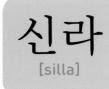

Between 57 BC-AD 935

The Silla Kingdom had lasted for almost 1000 years. It was the first unified kingdom on the Korean Peninsula. Gyeongju, the capital at the time, is now very popular among tourists for its wonderful antiquities.

## 06 The Address Order

| | | |
|---|---|---|
| Country | ▶ | 대한민국* [daehanminguk] |
| Province/City (or the Special City) | ▶ | 서울특별시 [seoulteukbyeolsi] |
| District | ▶ | 용산구 [yongsan-gu] |
| Street | ▶ | 한강로 2가 [hangangno-i-ga] |
| Lot | ▶ | 191번지 [baekgusibil beonji] |
| Building and floor | ▶ | 국제빌딩 19층 [gukjebilding sipgucheung] |
| Company name | ▶ | 삼일 C&L [samil ssienel] |
| Title and name | ▶ | 이사 이동구 [isa idonggu] |

| | | |
|---|---|---|
| Country | ▶ | 대한민국 [daehanminguk] |
| Province | ▶ | 경상남도 [gyeongsangnam-do] |
| City | ▶ | 진해시 [jinhae-si] |
| Village | ▶ | 여좌동 [yeojwa-dong] |
| House | ▶ | 63번지 [yuksipsam beonji] |
| Name | ▶ | 홍길동 [honggildong] |

It goes from the largest administrative unit to smaller ones, and then to the party's name.

＊대한민국 : The Republic of Korea

| Father | ▶ | 아버지 [abeoji] |
| Mother | ▶ | 어머니 [eomeoni] |
| Grandfather | ▶ | 할아버지 [harabeoji] |
| Grandmother | ▶ | 할머니 [halmeoni] |
| Elder brother | ▶ | 형 [hyeong] / 오빠 [oppa] |
| Younger brother | ▶ | 남동생 [namdongsaeng] |
| Elder sister | ▶ | 누나 [nuna] / 언니 [eonni] |
| Younger sister | ▶ | 여동생 [yeodongsaeng] |
| Company | ▶ | 회사 [hoesa] |
| President | ▶ | 사장 [sajang] |
| Executive | ▶ | 임원 [imwon] |
| Employee | ▶ | 사원 [sawon] |
| Regulations | ▶ | 규칙 [gyuchik] |
| Headquarters | ▶ | 본사 [bonsa] |
| Branch office | ▶ | 지사 [jisa] |

| | | |
|---|---|---|
| USA | ▶ | 미국 [miguk] |
| UK | ▶ | 영국 [yeongguk] |
| France | ▶ | 프랑스 [peurangseu] |
| Germany | ▶ | 독일 [dogil] |
| Russia | ▶ | 러시아 [reosia] |
| Japan | ▶ | 일본 [ilbon] |
| New York | ▶ | 뉴욕 [nyuyok] |
| London | ▶ | 런던 [reondeon] |
| Paris | ▶ | 파리 [pari] |
| Berlin | ▶ | 베를린 [bereullin] |
| Moscow | ▶ | 모스크바 [moseukeuba] |
| Tokyo | ▶ | 도쿄 [dokyo] |

The three main dishes make up a meal:

Has three meanings:

1. The main dish
2. Rice
3. The meal itself ( **i.e.** breakfast, lunch and
   dinner)

Soup

Side dishes

\* 김치: Kimchi (pickled vegetables)

# 수저 [sujeo] : the spoons and the chopsticks

\* A common meal would include a bowl of white rice, a few
  small side dishes and a bowl of soup.

\* Kimchi is the most popular side dish.

\* Some of the most popular spices include red peppers, sesame
  oil, soy sauce and garlic.

\* The Koreans, unlike the Japanese or Chinese, eat steamed
  (sticky) rice and soup using a spoon.

## 서울

Seoul - The Capital

Populated with approximately 10 million people (a quarter of the entire population of South Korea).

## 부산

Busan

Located in the southeast—the largest harbor city.

## 대구

Daegu

Located north of Busan—the third largest city in Korea.

# 대전, 광주, 경주
(Daejeon)   (Gwangju)   (Gyeongju)

**태극기**
[taegeukgi]

Taegeukgi

The National Flag

**무궁화**
[mugunghwa]

The Rose of Sharon

The National Flower

**까치**
[kkachi]

Magpie

The National Bird

Korea is also known as **The Land of Morning Calm** (조선).
[joseon]

## 06 Army Ranks

|  |  |
|---|---|
| General | ▶ 대장 [daejang] |
| Lieutenant General | ▶ 중장 [jungjang] |
| Major General | ▶ 소장 [sojang] |
| Brigadier General | ▶ 준장 [junjang] |
| Colonel | ▶ 대령 [daeryeong] |
| Lieutenant Colonel | ▶ 중령 [jungryeong] |
| Major | ▶ 소령 [soryeong] |
| Captain | ▶ 대위 [daewi] |
| 1st Lieutenant | ▶ 중위 [jung-wi] |
| 2nd Lieutenant | ▶ 소위 [sowi] |
| Warrant Officer | ▶ 준위 [junwi] |
| Master Sergeant | ▶ 상사 [sangsa] |
| Sergeant 1st Class | ▶ 중사 [jungsa] |
| Step Sergeant | ▶ 하사 [hasa] |
| Sergeant | ▶ 병장 [byeongjang] |
| Corporal | ▶ 상병 [sangbyeong] |
| Private First Class | ▶ 일등병 [ildeungbyeong] |
| Private | ▶ 이등병 [ideungbyeong] |

| Elementary School | ▶ | 초등학교 [chodeunghakgyo] |

| Middle School | ▶ | 중(등)학교 [jung(deung)hakgyo] |

| High School | ▶ | 고등학교 [godeunghakgyo] |

| University or College | ▶ | 대학교 [daehakgyo] |

**Note**

"학교" means *school*.　　"초등" means *primary grades*.

"중" means *middle grades*.　　"고등" means *high grades*.

"대" means *great*.

| 띠 | | | Year of Birth | | | |
|---|---|---|---|---|---|---|
| 쥐 [jwi] | Mouse | ▶ | '84 | '72 | '60 | '48 |
| 소 [so] | Ox (Cow) | ▶ | '85 | '73 | '61 | '49 |
| 호랑이 [horangi] | Tiger | ▶ | '86 | '74 | '62 | '50 |
| 토끼 [tokki] | Rabbit | ▶ | '87 | '75 | '63 | '51 |
| 용 [yong] | Dragon | ▶ | '88 | '76 | '64 | '52 |
| 뱀 [baem] | Snake | ▶ | '89 | '77 | '65 | '53 |
| 말 [mal] | Horse | ▶ | '90 | '78 | '66 | '54 |
| 양 [yang] | Sheep | ▶ | '91 | '79 | '67 | '55 |
| 원숭이 [wonsungi] | Monkey | ▶ | '92 | '80 | '68 | '56 |
| 닭 [dak] | Cock | ▶ | '93 | '81 | '69 | '57 |
| 개 [gae] | Dog | ▶ | '94 | '82 | '70 | '58 |
| 돼지 [dwaeji] | Pig | ▶ | '95 | '83 | '71 | '59 |

\* Each year has its own animal (e.g. 1980 is the year of the Monkey).

| | | |
|---|---|---|
| Bus | ▶ | 버스 [beoseu] |
| Taxi | ▶ | 택시 [taeksi] |
| Automobile | ▶ | 자동차 [jadongcha] |
| Train | ▶ | 기차 [gicha] |
| Subway | ▶ | 지하철 [jihacheol] |
| Motorcycle | ▶ | 오토바이 [otobai] |
| Bicycle | ▶ | 자전거 [jajeongeo] |
| Airplane | ▶ | 비행기 [bihaenggi] |
| Ship/Boat | ▶ | 배 [bae] |
| Ticket | ▶ | 표 [pyo] |
| Fare/Charge | ▶ | 운임 [unim] |

## 06 Drinks

| 1. 탄산음료 | | Soft Drinks (Soda) |
|---|---|---|
| 콜라 [colla] | ▶ | Coke |
| 사이다 [saida] | ▶ | 7UP/Sprite |
| 오렌지주스 [orenji juseu] | ▶ | Orange Juice |
| 물 [mul] | ▶ | Water |
| 광천수 [gwangcheonsu] | ▶ | Mineral/Spring Water |

| 2. 술 | | Liquors |
|---|---|---|
| 맥주 [maekju] | ▶ | Beer |
| 스카치 [seukachi] | ▶ | Scotch |
| 브랜디 [beuraendi] | ▶ | Brandy |
| 정종/사케 [jeongjong/sake] | ▶ | Sake |
| 럼 [reom] | ▶ | Rum |
| 백포도주 [baekpodoju] | ▶ | White Wine |
| 적포도주 [jeokpodoju] | ▶ | Red Wine |
| 소주 [soju] | ▶ | *Soju* (distilled liquor) |

## Utilities 06

## 1. Electric Power Unit

**Voltage** : AC 220 V at 60 Hz
**Outlet** : Plugs with round tips

May work with some European models but not with American or Japanese ones.

## 2. Telephone Numbers

**Country code** : 82
**Area codes (omit 0 when dialing overseas)**
서울 (Seoul) : 02
부산 (Busan) : 051
대전 (Daejeon) : 052
대구 (Daegu) : 053

**Phone numbers** : Mostly three and four, or four and four digits
(e.g. 123-4567, 1234-5678)

| Here | ▶ | 여기 [yeogi] |
| There | ▶ | 저기 [jeogi] |
| Where | ▶ | 어디 [eodi] |
| Faraway | ▶ | 멀리 [meolli] |
| Near | ▶ | 가까이 [gakkai] |
| Right Side | ▶ | 오른쪽 [oreunjjok] |
| Left Side | ▶ | 왼쪽 [oenjjok] |
| Middle | ▶ | 가운데 [gaunde] |
| Forward | ▶ | 앞으로 [apeuro] |
| Backward | ▶ | 뒤로 [dwiro] |
| Upward | ▶ | 위로 [wiro] |
| Downward | ▶ | 아래로 [araero] |

# Formulating Sentences

# 07 The Ground Rules of Word Order

- English : I am going to school.

- Korean : 나 는 학교 에 갑니다.
  [ na neun hakgyo - e gamnida ]

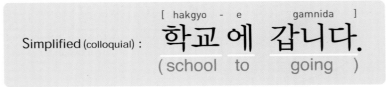

Simplified (colloquial) :
[ hakgyo - e gamnida ]
학교 에 갑니다.
( school to going )

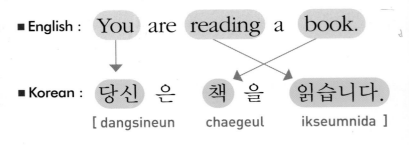

- English : You are reading a book.

- Korean : 당신 은 책 을 읽습니다.
  [ dangsineun chaegeul ikseumnida ]

Simplified (colloquial) :
[ chaegeul ikseumnida ]
책 을 읽습니다.
(book reading )

106

**A**

[ hakgyo-e     gamnida ]

학교에     갑니<u>다</u>.

school to     going

**I**

[ hakgyo-e     gamnikka ]

학교에     갑니<u>까</u>?

school to     going

**A**

[ chaegeul     ikseumnida ]

책을     읽습니<u>다</u>.

book     reading

**I**

[ chaegeul     ikseumnikka ]

책을     읽습니<u>까</u>?

book     reading

＊Interrogatives always have rising intonation.

**A**

[ jibe     gamnida ]

집에    갑니<u>다</u>.

home to   going

**I**

[ jibe     gamnikka ]

집에    갑니<u>까</u>?

home to   going

**A**

[ chingureul    mannamnida ]

친구를    만납니<u>다</u>.

friend      seeing

**I**

[ chingureul    mannamnikka ]

친구를    만납니<u>까</u>?

friend      seeing

✻ Interrogatives always have rising intonation.

| [ yeogi | chaegi | itseumnida ] |
|---------|--------|---------------|
| 여기 | 책이 | 있습니**다**. |
| here | book | there is |

| [ yeogi | chaegi | itseumnikka ] |
|---------|--------|----------------|
| 여기 | 책이 | 있습니**까**? |
| here | book | is there |

| [ jeogi | chaegi | itseumnida ] |
|---------|--------|---------------|
| 저기 | 책이 | 있습니**다**. |
| there | book | there is |

| [ jeogi | chaegi | itseumnikka ] |
|---------|--------|----------------|
| 저기 | 책이 | 있습니**까**? |
| there | book | is there |

| [ yeogi | chaegi | eopseumnida ] |
|---|---|---|
| 여기 | 책이 | 없습니**다**. |
| Here | book | there is no |

| [ yeogi | chaegi | eopseumnikka ] |
|---|---|---|
| 여기 | 책이 | 없습니**까**? |
| Here | book | is there no |

| [ jeogi | chaegi | eopseumnida ] |
|---|---|---|
| 저기 | 책이 | 없습니**다**. |
| There | book | there is no |

| [ jeogi | chaegi | eopseumnikka ] |
|---|---|---|
| 저기 | 책이 | 없습니**까**? |
| There | book | is there no |

| [ yeogi | keun | chaegi | itseumnida ] |
|---|---|---|---|
| 여기 | 큰 | 책이 | 있습니다. |
| Here | big | book | there is |

| [ yeogi | keun | chaegi | itseumnikka ] |
|---|---|---|---|
| 여기 | 큰 | 책이 | 있습니까? |
| Here | big | book | is there |

| [ jeogi | keun | chaegi | itseumnida ] |
|---|---|---|---|
| 저기 | 큰 | 책이 | 있습니다. |
| There | big | book | there is |

| [ jeogi | keun | chaegi | itseumnikka ] |
|---|---|---|---|
| 저기 | 큰 | 책이 | 있습니까? |
| There | big | book | is there |

| [ yeogi | jageun | chaegi | itseumnida ] |
|---------|--------|--------|--------------|
| 여기 | 작은 | 책이 | 있습니다. |
| Here | small | book | there is |

| [ yeogi | jageun | chaegi | itseumnikka ] |
|---------|--------|--------|---------------|
| 여기 | 작은 | 책이 | 있습니까? |
| Here | small | book | is there |

| [ jeogi | jageun | chaegi | itseumnida ] |
|---------|--------|--------|--------------|
| 저기 | 작은 | 책이 | 있습니다. |
| There | small | book | there is |

| [ jeogi | jageun | chaegi | itseumnikka ] |
|---------|--------|--------|---------------|
| 저기 | 작은 | 책이 | 있습니까? |
| There | small | book | is there |

| This | 이것 | → | [ igeot ] |
| That | 저것 | → | [ jeogeot ] |
| How much | 얼마 | → | [ eolma ] |
| The big one | 큰 것 | → | [ keun geot ] |
| The small one | 작은 것 | → | [ jageun geot ] |

## How much is this?

이것은    얼마    입니까?

this    how much    is

[ igeoseun    eolma    imnikka ]

*입니까? : Interrogative

**Q** How much is this?

이것은 얼마 입니까?

[ igeoseun eolmaimnikka ]

**A** That is 100 dollars.

그것은 백 달러 입니다.

[ geugeoseun baekdalleoimnida ]

It's too expensive.

너무 비쌉니다.

[ neomu bissamnida ]

Can you offer me a little cheaper one?

조금 싼 것으로 주시겠습니까?

[ jogeum ssan geoseuro jusigetseumnikka ]

| To school, | Go (-ing). | / | Go (-ing) ? |
|---|---|---|---|

학교에,
[ hakgyo-e ]

갑니다. / 갑니까?
[gamnida] [gamnikka]

간다. / 가니?
[ganda] [gani]

가십니다. / 가십니까?
[gasimnida] [gasimnikka]

---

갑니다 : Formal

(갑니까?) : Used with strangers

- - - - - - - - - - - - - - - - - - - - - - -

간다 : Informal or casual

(가니?) : Used with close friends

- - - - - - - - - - - - - - - - - - - - - - -

가십니다 : Honorific

(가십니까?) : Used with people of authority
and with much older people

(e.g. parents, teachers, superiors, etc.)

# 안녕하십니까?

[ annyeonghasimnikka ]

- Meaning : Are you alright? Are you happy and healthy ?
- Use : Greetings
  - Good morning.
  - Good afternoon.
  - How are you?
  - Hello/Hi.

*"안녕 [annyeong]" is the key word : "Happy and Healthy"

# 안녕히 가십시오.

[ annyeonghi gasipsio ]

- Meaning : Please have a safe and peaceful journey.
- Use : Saying good-byes

# **Appendix** (FORMULAS)

1. 14 consonants &
   10 vowels, each with
   their own sound values
   Let's say, consonants
   stand for men and vowels
   stand for women.

| | | | |
|---|---|---|---|
| ㄱ | g/k | ㅏ | a |
| ㄴ | n | ㅑ | ya |
| ㄷ | d | ㅓ | eo |
| ㄹ | r/l | ㅕ | yeo |
| ㅁ | m | ㅗ | o |
| ㅂ | b/p | ㅛ | yo |
| ㅅ | s | ㅜ | u |
| ㅇ | (ZERO) | ㅠ | yu |
| ㅈ | j | ㅡ | eu |
| ㅊ | ch | ㅣ | i |
| ㅋ | k | | |
| ㅌ | t | | |
| ㅍ | p | | |
| ㅎ | h | | |

2. **The words are made up by the combinations
   of consonants (men) and vowels (women).**

   2-1 A man and a woman get married and become a family.

   2-2 A man may have 2 or 3 wives.

   2-3 A woman may likewise have 2 husbands.

   2-4 A given two men may have two wives.

   2-5 A man (consonant) always comes before and/or
       lies over everyone else.

   2-5-1 A man (consonant) should come before his wife
         when she stands up.

   2-5-2 A man (consonant) should lie over his wife
         when she lies down.

3. **Some people may prefer sons.**

   3-1 A son always follows his parents.

   3-1-1 Father (man) comes before, Mother (woman) after.
         Then the son follows.

   3-1-2 Some families may have twins.

# Korean Crossword Puzzle

| 1 | | 7 | | | | 10 | |
|---|---|---|---|---|---|----|---|
| | | | | | | | |
| | | | | | | 2 | |
| | | | | | 3 | | |
| | | | 9 | | | 4 | |
| 5 | | 8 | | | | | |
| | | | | | | | |
| | | 6 | | | | | |

# 가로 (horizontal)

1. Hangeul was created by <u>this king</u> during his reign in the 15th century.
2. a branch office
3. a distilled alcohol beverage made from rice which is native to Korea
4. 20 in pure Korean
5. "Diana" in Korean
6. subway

# 세로 (vertical)

7. The Republic of Korea
8. father
9. a boy's older sister
10. orange juice

# Answer

|   |   |   |   |   |   |   |   |
|---|---|---|---|---|---|---|---|
| ¹세 | 종 | ⁷대 | 왕 |   |   | ¹⁰오 |   |
|   |   | 한 |   |   |   | 렌 |   |
|   |   | 민 |   |   |   | ²지 | 사 |
|   |   | 국 |   |   | ³소 | 주 |   |
|   |   |   | ⁹누 |   |   | ⁴스 | 물 |
| ⁵다 | 이 | ⁸아 | 나 |   |   |   |   |
|   |   | 버 |   |   |   |   |   |
|   |   | ⁶지 | 하 | 철 |   |   |   |

120